What Happens When You Go to the Hospital

by Arthur Shay

REILLY & LEE · CHICAGO

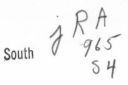
Other books by Arthur Shay:

WHAT HAPPENS WHEN YOU MAIL A LETTER

WHAT HAPPENS WHEN YOU PUT MONEY IN THE BANK

WHAT HAPPENS WHEN YOU MAKE A TELEPHONE CALL

WHAT HAPPENS WHEN YOU TRAVEL BY PLANE

WHAT HAPPENS IN A CAR FACTORY

**For Bertha Herz,
the youngest eighty year old in the world**

To Parents and Teachers

Hospitals have long been mysterious places to children. They know mothers go there to bring home new babies and that people are made well there. They also know that children aren't allowed past the waiting room as visitors.

When a child does go to the hospital it is usually for a tonsilectomy or other surgery, to have a broken bone set, or for any of the myriad trauma of childhood. Having seen the hospital through tears too many children tend to view hospitals with awe, and even worse, with fear.

In this book I hope to dispel some of the fear and unveil some of the mysteries by showing children that nearly everything that goes on behind hospital walls is adjunctive to the miracle of healing.

In addition I hope this book will teach children something about the jobs and services, subsidiary to medicine, performed in a hospital.

I wish to thank St. Joseph's Hospital of Joliet, Illinois for its hospitality, Karen Mitchell for being such a good patient even when it hurt, and St. Joseph's Public Relations Director Charles Stroud for his help in arranging for the usually forbidden camera to enter the hospital. I would also like to thank Astra Photo Laboratory of Chicago for their darkroom skills.

Arthur Shay

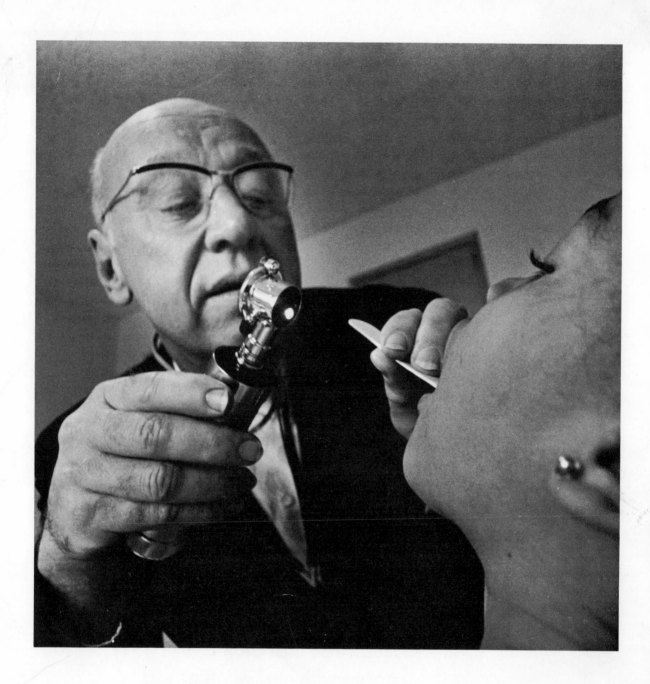

One day Karen Mitchell's doctor noticed that Karen's tonsils were a little too large and swollen. "It looks to me as if those tonsils should come out," he said. "This means you'll have to spend two days in the hospital, Karen." Karen looked frightened. She wasn't sure she wanted to go to a hospital, but she would try to be brave.

At the hospital, Karen's parents filled out a long form all about Karen: her age, whether there were medicines that didn't agree with her, whether she had ever had measles, mumps, chicken pox, and some other diseases Karen had never heard of in her life.

Karen got to sign her own name, too. She became patient 139,059.

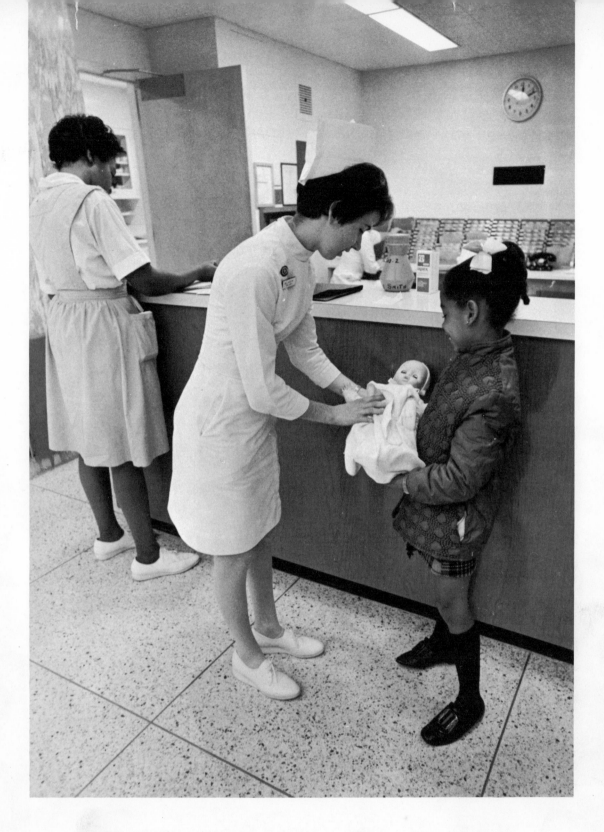

Then, Karen, her parents, and Karen's doll,
named Susie, went to the fifth floor, where Karen
was to stay. She met her nurse, Joyce Quigley,
who takes care of boys and girls in the hospital.

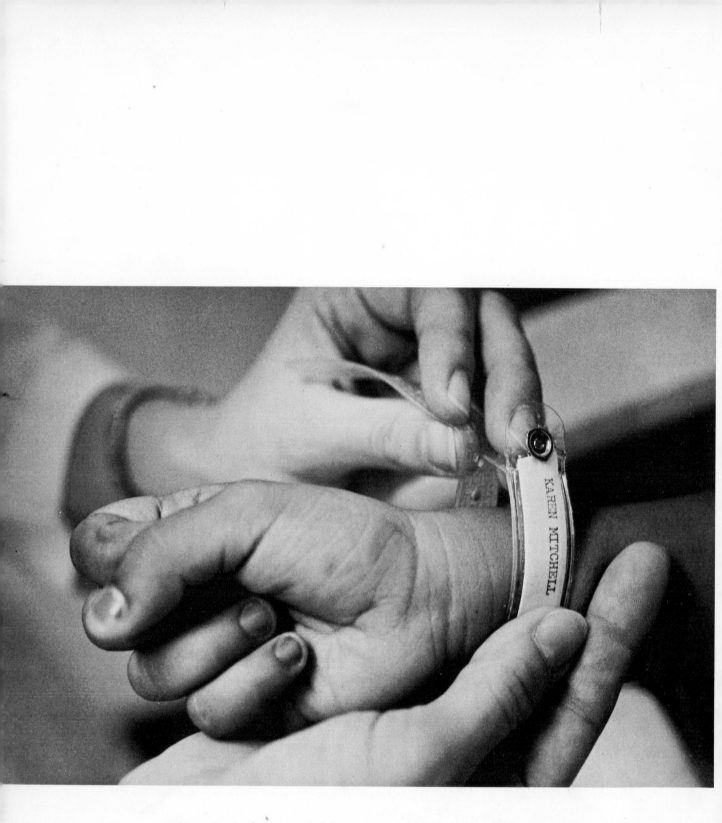

Miss Quigley quickly typed Karen's name on a
small card, put it into a plastic bracelet, and
placed it on Karen's wrist like a wristwatch.
Hospitals use wristbands, so you can't get lost.
Everyone knows who you are, even if you're sleeping.

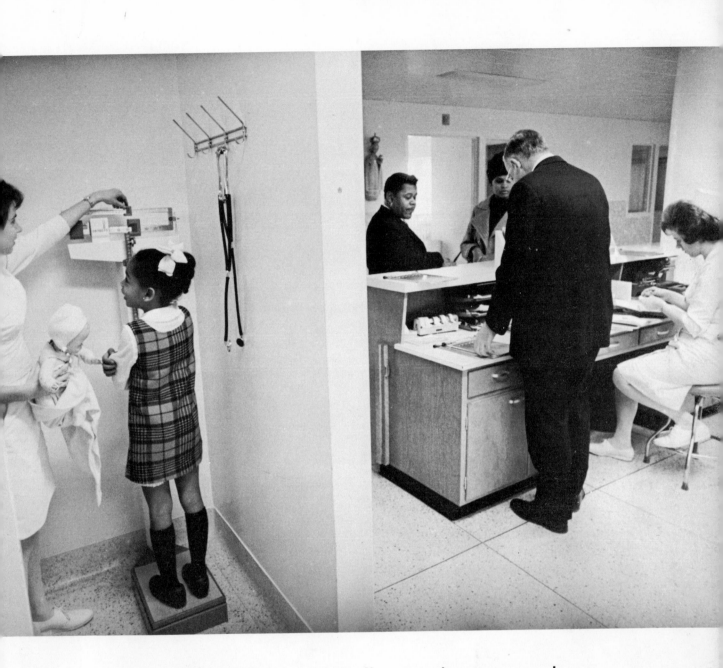

While Mr. and Mrs. Mitchell gave the nurse and
the doctor some more information about Karen,
Miss Quigley weighed Karen. Karen weighed
fifty-one pounds. Then Karen weighed Susie.
Susie weighed half a pound.

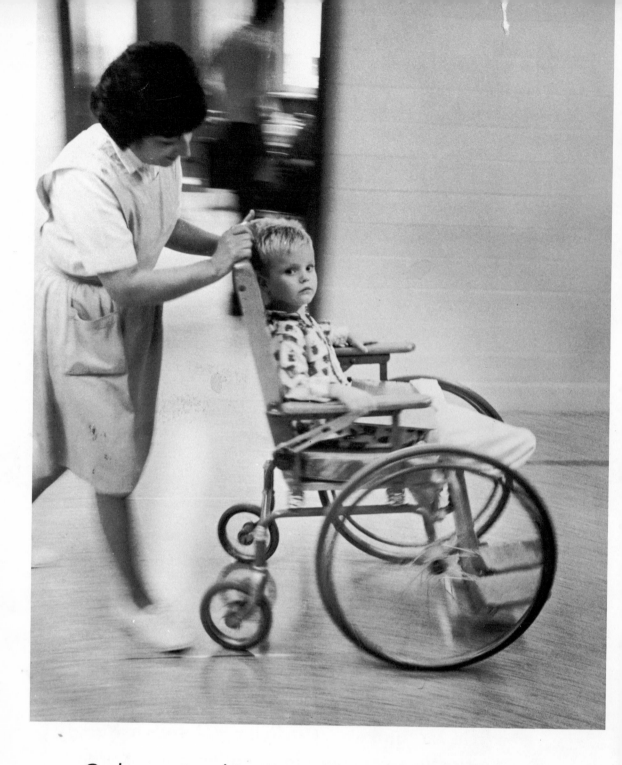

On her way to her room, Karen saw a nurse's helper, called a nurse's aide, pushing a boy in a wheel chair.

"He has a broken ankle that's healing nicely," said Miss Quigley. "They're on their way to the playroom. Would you like to see it, Karen? It's on our way."

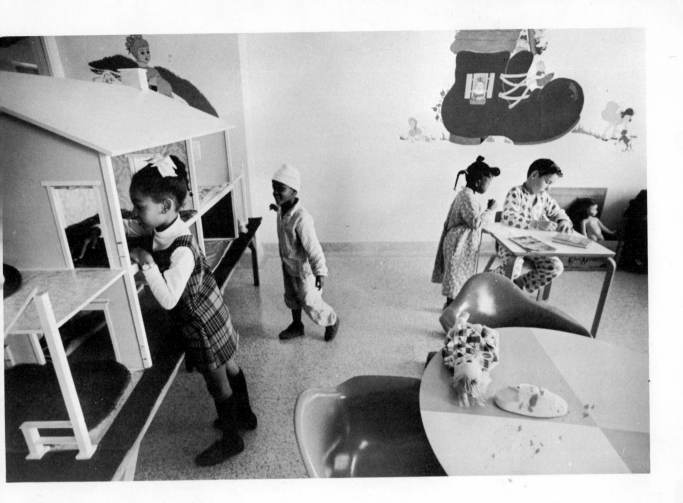

In the playroom Karen met other children who were staying in the hospital, but who didn't have to stay in bed all the time. There were lots of toys to play with and even a television set.

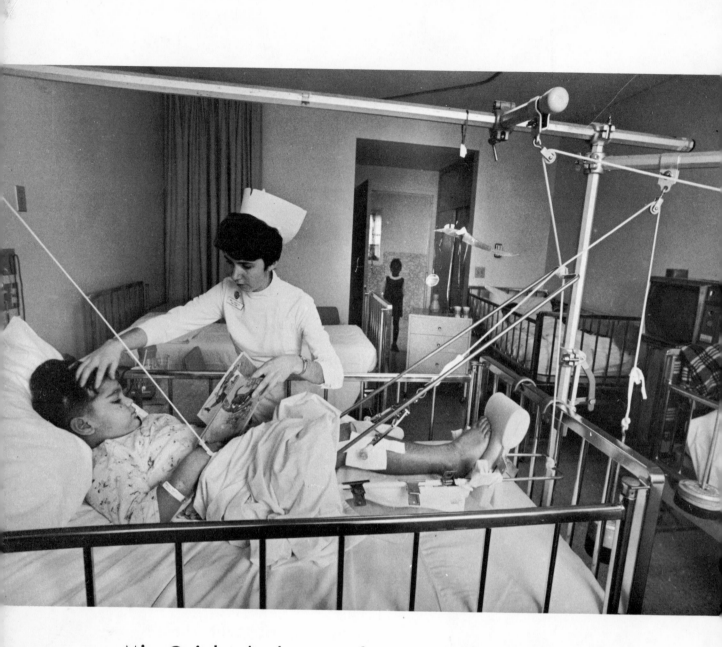

Miss Quigley had to stop for a moment to help another one of her patients, Angelo, who was in traction.

Traction keeps bones still and straight while they heal. Angelo was hit by a car which broke his hip and leg, but he will be as good as new after awhile.

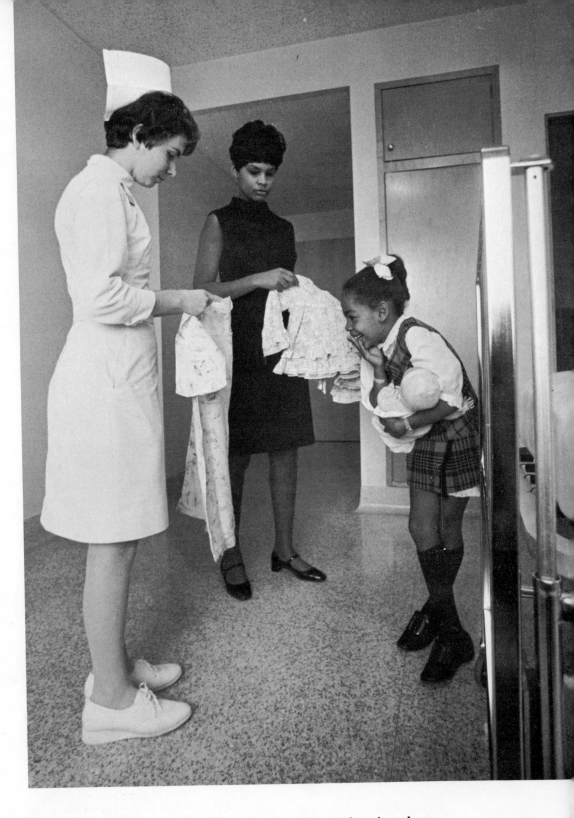

Just next door was Karen's room. She had to
choose which to wear: her own pajamas or the
hospital gown. She chose the hospital gown.

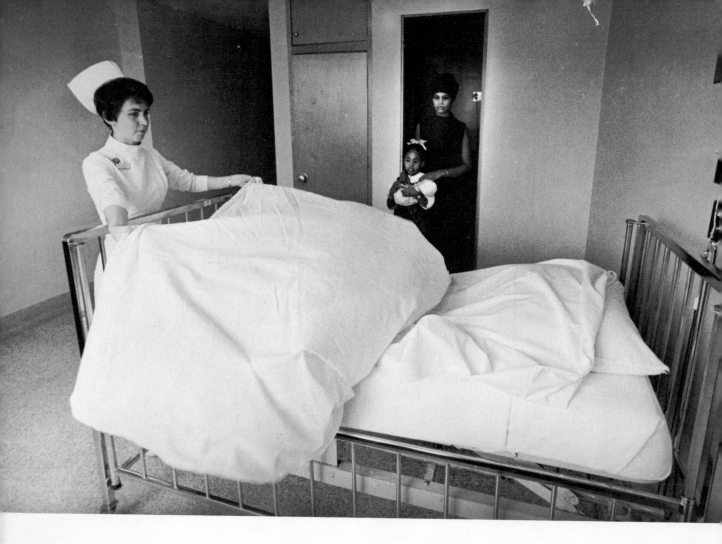

Before she put on the gown,
Karen watched Miss Quigley
make the bed. Miss Quigley
told Karen that she had made
hundreds of beds, and that the
hospital laundry washed and
ironed thousands of sheets,
pillowcases, and nightgowns every
day.

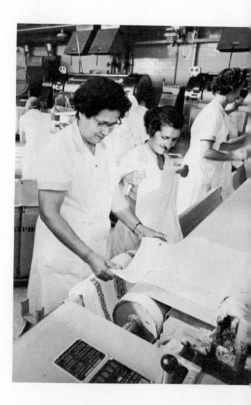

One of the first things Karen learned was how to call for her nurse in case she needed something. All she had to do was pull a string. The string turned on three lights: one over her head, one in the hall over her door, and one at the nurses' station. Her nurse would be sure to see one of the lights.

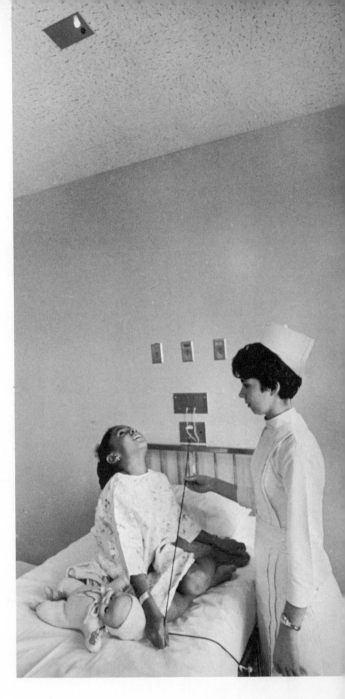

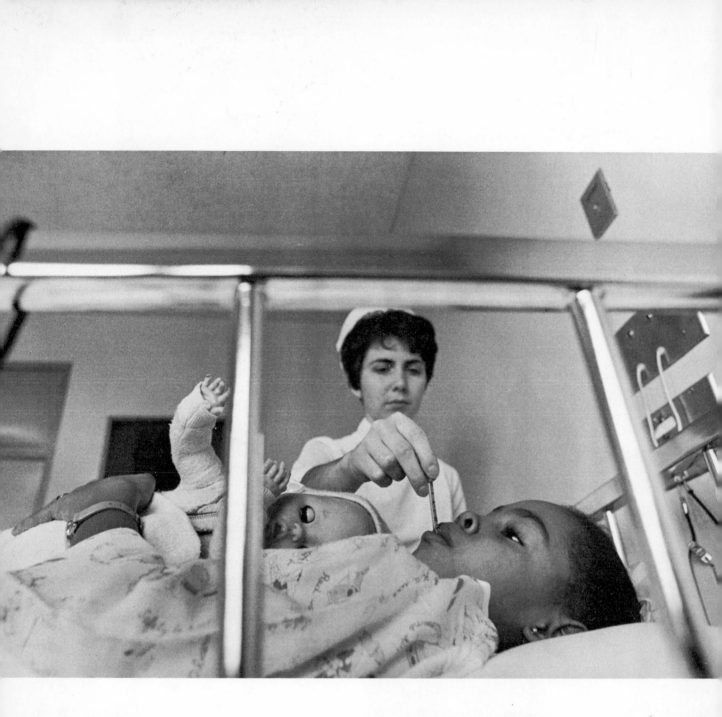

At first Karen wasn't sure she liked her hospital bed, because it had sides on it like a crib. Before she found out that the sides were for safety, and before she could worry about it, Miss Quigley came in and popped a thermometer into Karen's mouth.

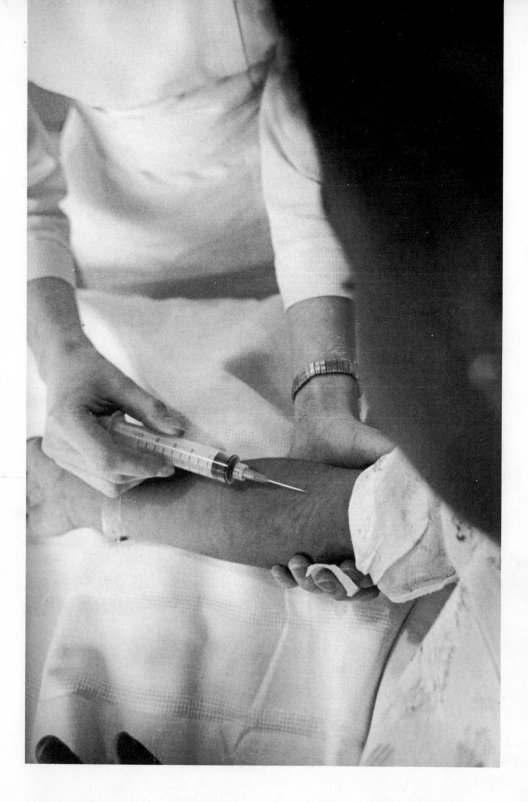

Next Karen had a blood test to see if she was healthy. The nurse pricked Karen's arm with a hollow needle and drew some of her blood into a small glass tube to take to the laboratory. Karen was frightened, but she didn't cry.

"It's the opposite of a shot, isn't it?" Karen said bravely.

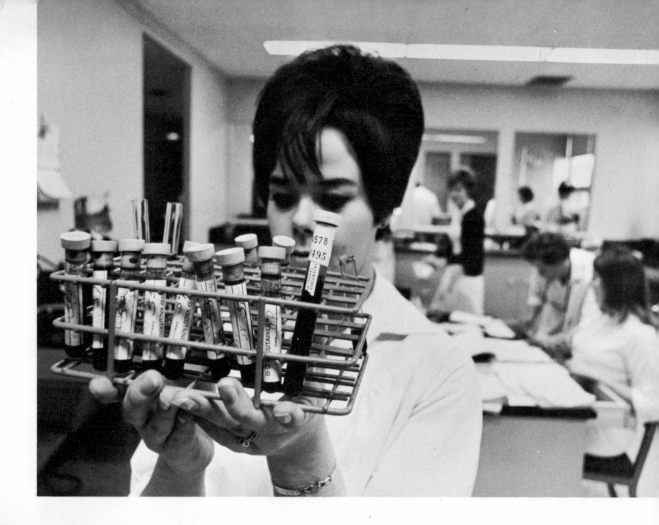

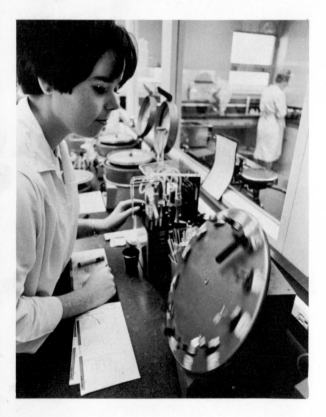

Karen's blood sample was taken to the laboratory, along with a sample of her urine, for testing. The people who work in the laboratory are called lab technicians. They put a number on Karen's blood sample; it was 578,495. They whirled the tube of blood around like a phonograph record, which mixed the blood so that they could make their tests.

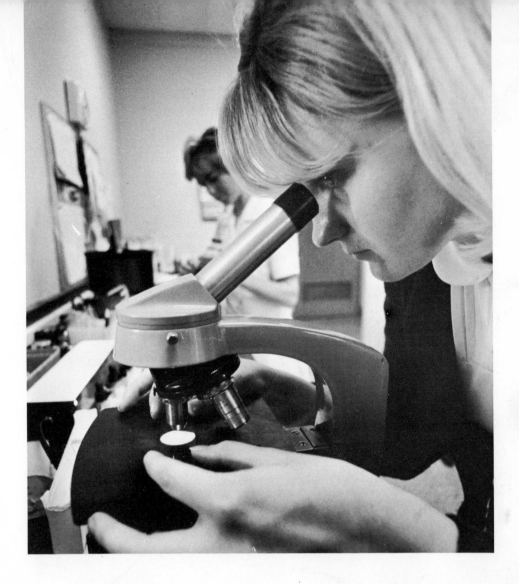

When a lab technician
looked at Karen's blood
through a microscope,
she found it was healthy
as could be.

Another lab technician
tested a small sample of
Karen's urine from a
paper cup. This is another
way to tell if a person is
healthy.

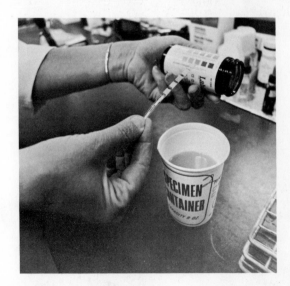

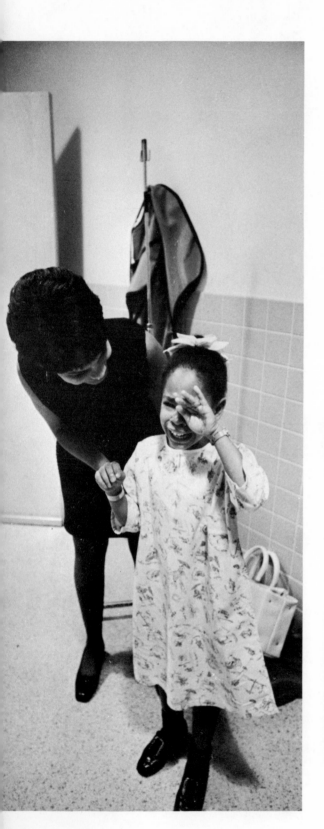

One of the hospital rules
is that every patient
must have a chest X-ray.
Karen didn't like the
X-ray machine, but she
stopped crying when she
saw a boy smile while
having his foot X-rayed.

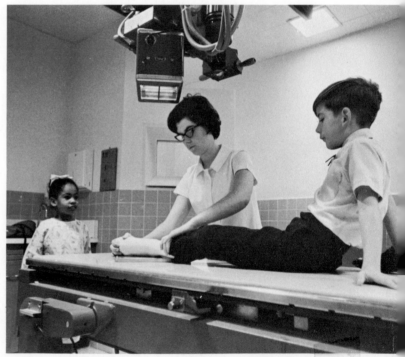

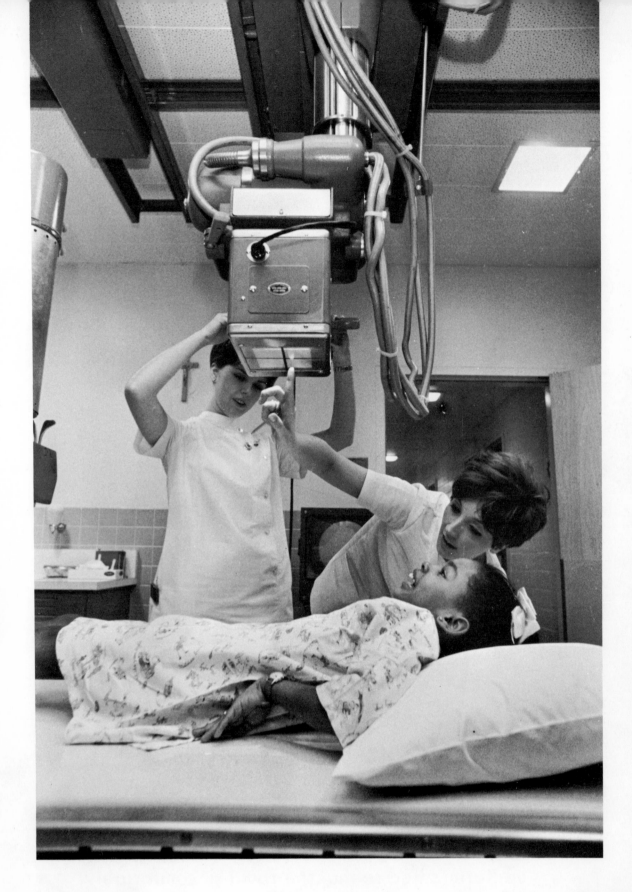

"It didn't hurt," she said. "The machine just made a funny noise."

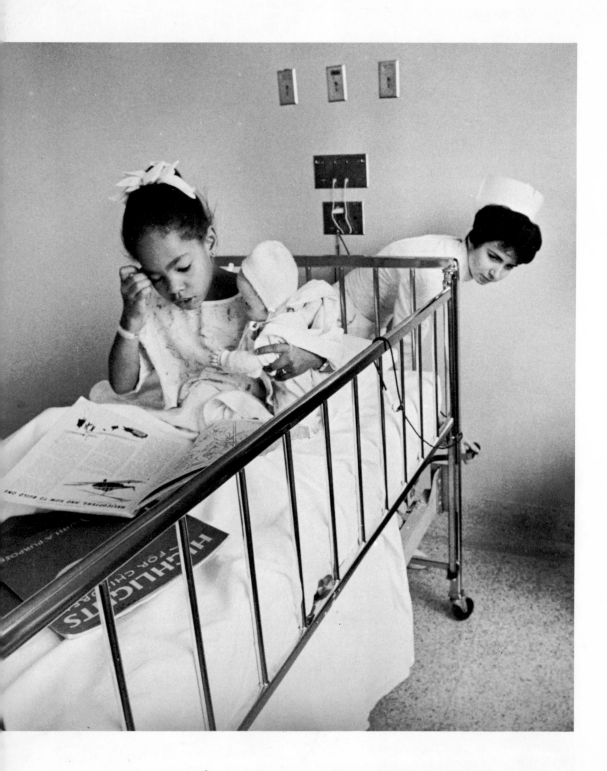

It was almost supper time. Miss Quigley cranked up Karen's bed so that she could sit comfortably.

Soon an announcement from the loudspeakers told all visitors that the visiting hours were over. An operator at the telephone switchboard makes announcements. She also calls for doctors who are needed.

Karen cried a little when her parents said good-bye. Her father said, "Don't worry. We'll take you home a few hours after your tonsils are taken out."

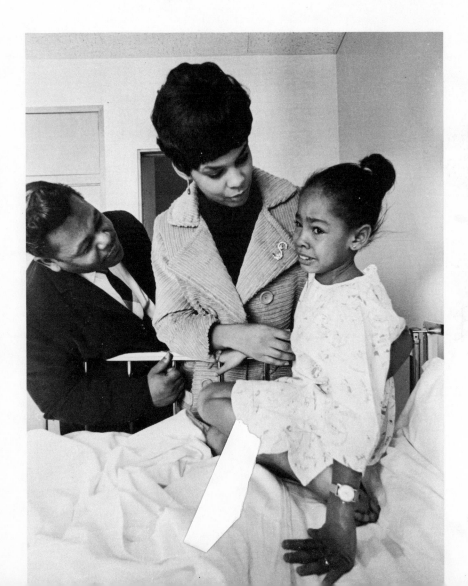

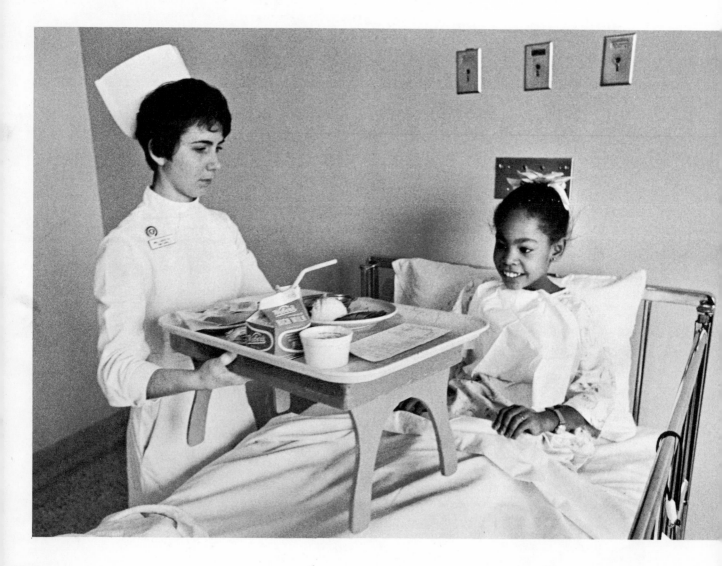

Miss Quigley came in with a small tray filled
with roast beef, mashed potatoes, milk, and
jello. "You'd better eat it all," said the nurse.
"You won't be allowed to eat before your tonsils
come out in the morning."

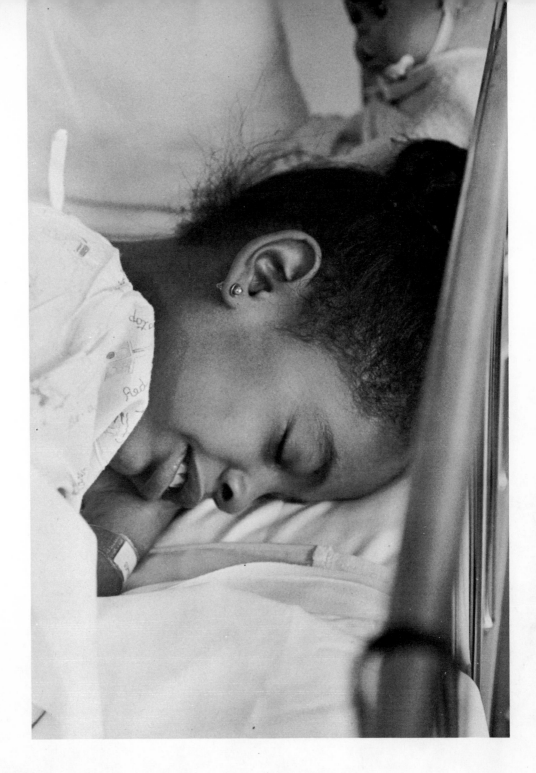

Karen read for a little while after supper,
played nurse to Susie, and then went to sleep. Her
big day would start at 7 A.M. Even though Karen
slept soundly all night and didn't pull the string,
several nurses looked in during the night to make
sure she was all right.

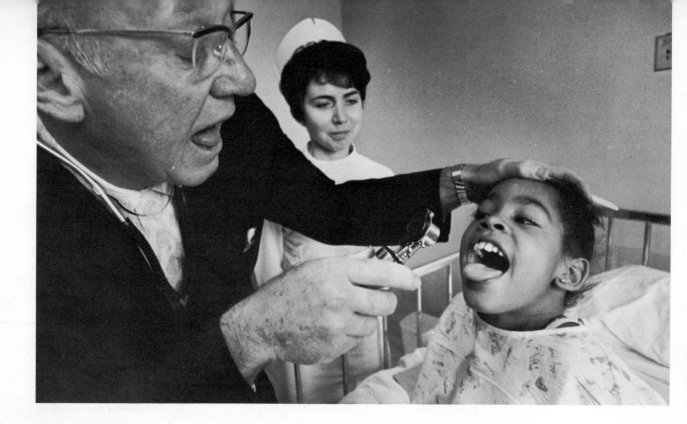

The next day her doctor and her nurse came in
to make absolutely sure that Karen's tonsils
were ready to come out.

Karen was given a shot, which put her to sleep.
Then, her nurse took her on a cart in an elevator
to the operating room.

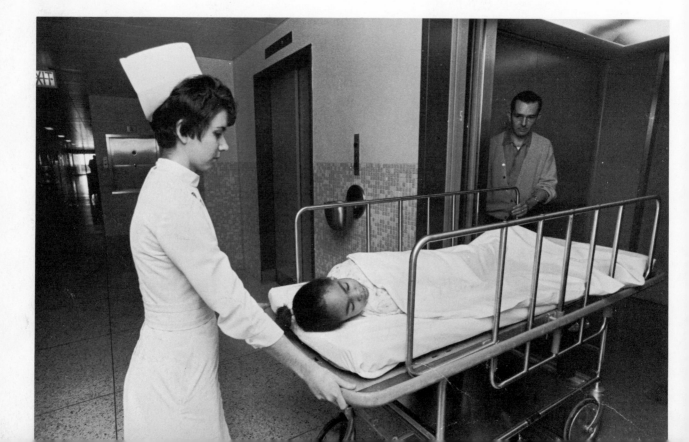

In the operating room the doctor removed
Karen's tonsils, but Karen didn't feel anything at
all because she was fast asleep!

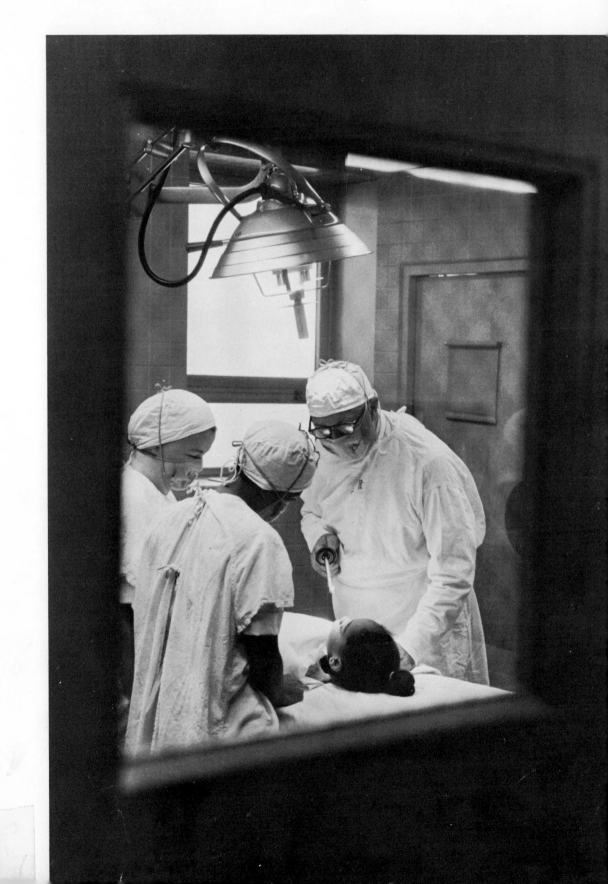

When Karen woke up in the recovery room, one
of the nurse's aides showed her the tonsils.

Later Miss Quigley gave
her some ice water to
make her throat feel
better. Then she got to
eat all the ice cream she
wanted!

After a short nap, Karen was almost ready to leave the hospital. She said good-bye to her friends at the hospital, got dressed and packed.

While her father paid the bill, Karen saw a man and a woman leaving the hospital with their new baby.

In a few minutes Mr. and Mrs. Mitchell and Karen, less one pair of annoying tonsils, were on their way home.

"Hey," said Karen, "My wristband will be perfect for show and tell!"